The Crazy Inside

by

Alicia Birmingham

Edited by: D. Rosnick

Graphic Design by: Heather Wood

This book is dedicated to my family and friends who are one and the same. You know who you are.

"Families are like fudge, mostly sweet,
with a few nuts."
-Unknown

The following is a poetic non-fiction, the story of my frenzied years suffering with bipolar disorder.

ACKNOWLEDGEMENTS

I'd like to thank those whose talent and patience helped
make this book possible: Heather Wood, Joe Kovach,
D. Rosnick, Jason Bowman, Chris Urban, Rachel Rosnick,
Valerie Ott, Brandon Hatfield, Jason Pope, Justin Ross,
The Vandals, Sing the Evens, Play the Odds, Shiver,
The Relapse, Marilyn Jean Wood, Ron Pederson,
Tim Seitz and John E. Bodnar

Before you turn the page and enter The Crazy Inside

Years ago when I wrote gig reviews for a music criticism site, I would often get mail from readers around the world. One day about eight years ago, I received a letter, which because of the appreciation, support and even empathy expressed within it, I have never forgotten. This letter was written by Alicia Birmingham, who had been to some of the same punk gigs in Pittsburgh that I had reviewed.

Later, I would often see Alicia at shows. Sometimes, we would hang out before or after them, and it was during this time that I got to know her and witness her struggles. To say that I admired her strength of will and determination is an understatement. Through mania, hospitalizations, medication trial and errors and even while held in depression's relentless grasp, her spirit remained undaunted and was truly inspiring.

Now in remission, Alicia Birmingham's creativity shines through. In *The Crazy Inside*, she not only provides an honest, no-frills, unflinching view from *high atop Cardiac Hill*, but she also, through her vivid imagery, deftly reveals the redemptive power of poetry as she renders manic depression's mad, bad and dangerous moments into works of art.

I remember after one of her hospitalizations, Alicia sent me what she said were just some things from a journal she had kept while a patient at Western Psychiatric Hospital. She asked me to read them as she was thinking about doing something with them. At the time, she had been trying her hand at writing short stories and other types of prose, but nothing seemed to satisfy her need to create through writing what she wanted to express. After reading what she'd sent me from her journal, I told her that I liked her poems. She asked, "What poems? I don't write poetry. Those are just entries from my journal."

Sometimes even the most insightful of us fail to recognize our own gifts.

D. Rosnick

-Editor

"I'm well aware that you're chemically imbalanced"
-The Vandals

99

I let it get out of hand
One night I was crazy
wild
searching the streets for strangers
then letting that stranger live with me
steal my friend and
try to bring her house down in flames
At the time
it seemed like it all happened
in the blink of an eye
each day rushing past
Looking back
it was like every day
was longer than the next
every breath slow and deep
sucking in the time between sunrise and sunset
swallowing the golden rays that lined each cloud
This is the way time creeps by when you have insomnia
making it difficult to remember
what is real
and what is just going through the motions
You beg
You cry for release
for some time away from this world
and yet
it does
not
come

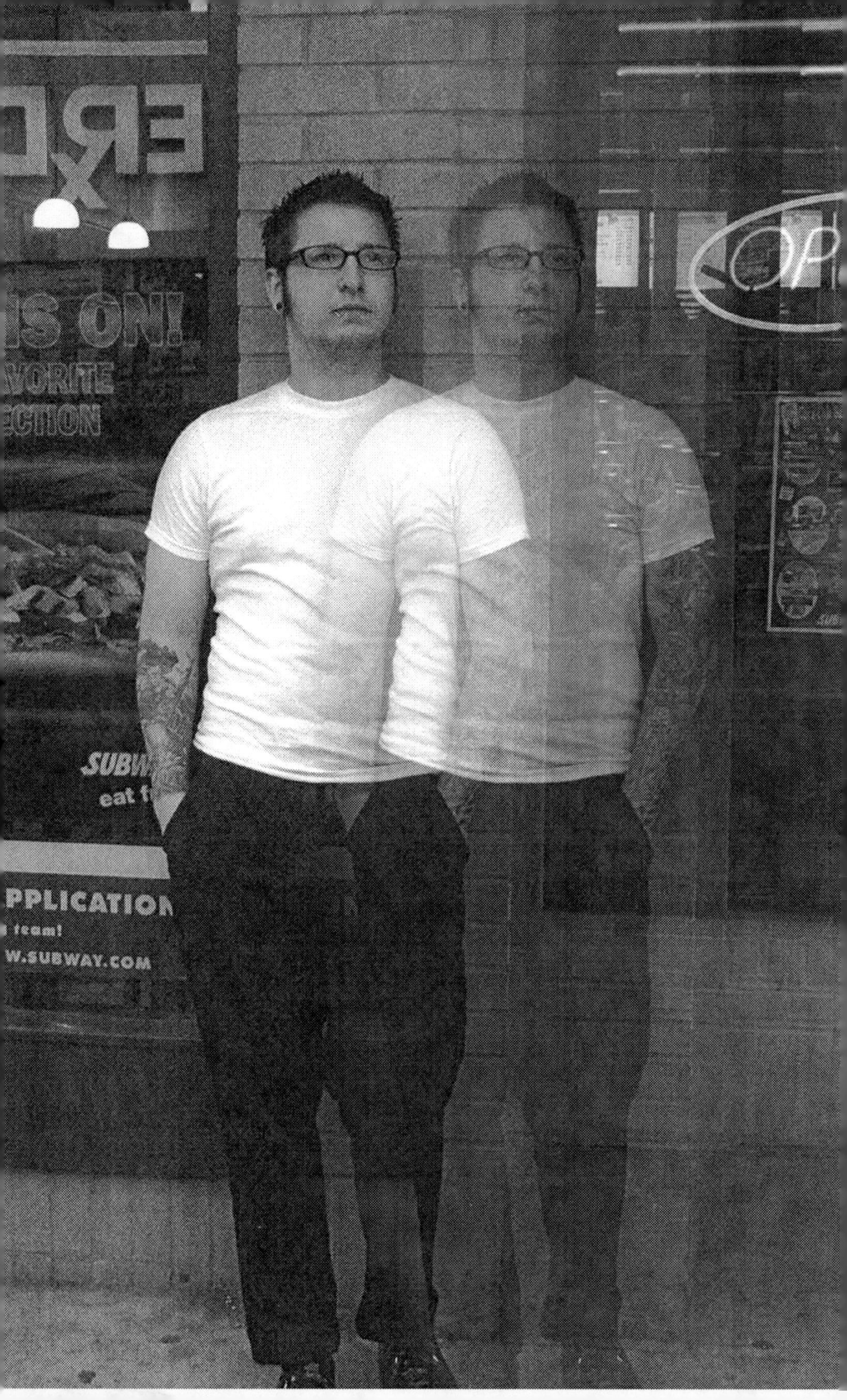

Killing the Suicide
(For Karrie)

1200 mgs of your favorite anti-psychotic
won't kill you
but it will make you fall on your face on Forbes Avenue
on your ass on Oakland Avenue
and totally incapacitate you right before you forget your name

This is what I think about
as I struggle towards sleep
my body begging for some
Geodon
Ativan
Restoril
while my mind races with thoughts of you

I wonder what floor you're on
There's a good chance I've been there
and walked those halls before you
staining the space with my pleasure
as they medicated my mania away

Tonight I committed you
to hide you
safe from yourself
I imagine you can see your house from there
You
taking your turn
enjoying your view
high atop Cardiac Hill
You
at the opposite end of my spectrum
depression eating away at your soul
Yet you fight
killing the suicide inside

photo credits: Jason Bowman

Insomnia

One day you wake up
and somehow you start living
fast and furious
and you
just
can't
stop

Reality comes
ripping at the seams
and your days are longer
and slower
than before

Walking
slack jaw
eyes red and weary
you beg for relief
for an escape from your
frantic
maniacal mind

Strangers

There's a charge
under my skin
while I walk the streets
searching for someone
anyone

Like a succubus
I drain them
from this existence
baring my soul
my body
to those whose names
are meaningless
Strangers
I suppose that's as close as I can get
I try desperately to connect
in the most intimate of ways
with people who tomorrow
won't remember my face

I tell my shadow
to wake me in the morning
so I can sneak back to my life
and leave these regrets far
far behind

photo credits: Jason Bowman

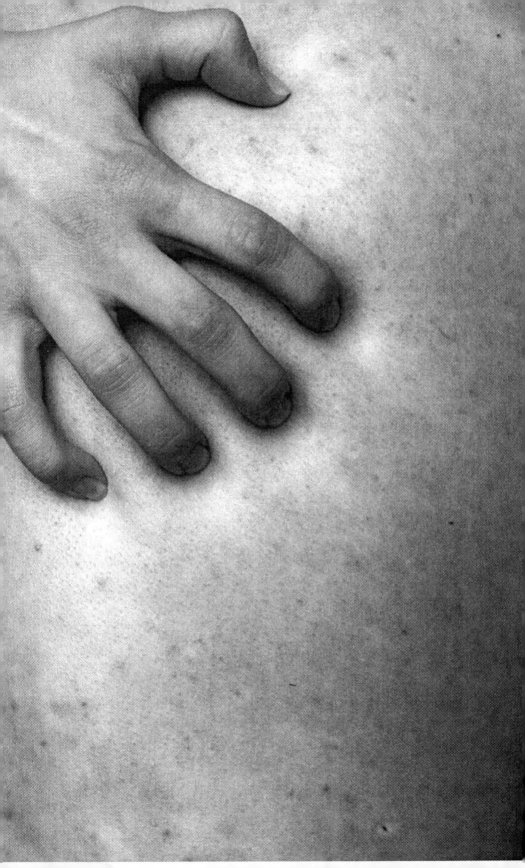

My Way

"I would give anything to see those tits,"
he said to me
while he drooled down my neck
wishing for a moment alone
a moment where he wouldn't have to think
about his wife
or two kids

My legs were shaking
as he caressed me under the table
saying
"Please, calm down. You are so beautiful."

He smelled like cheap beer
and cheap lines
but when the mania takes hold
this sounds like romance
and I don't mind
as long as someone is looking my way

Slide

At first the mania was like laughter on broken glass
Now it's more like razors along miles of silk

I've never felt happiness so smooth
like lips kissed with raspberry desire
My smile spreads across my face like butter

mood stabilizers
anti-psychotics
sedatives

I can claw my way out from all of them
my mind racing
static screeching
over the grey matter between my ears
sliding fast
gaining speed
on this slick Teflon highway
half formed thoughts slip away
before I can even touch them

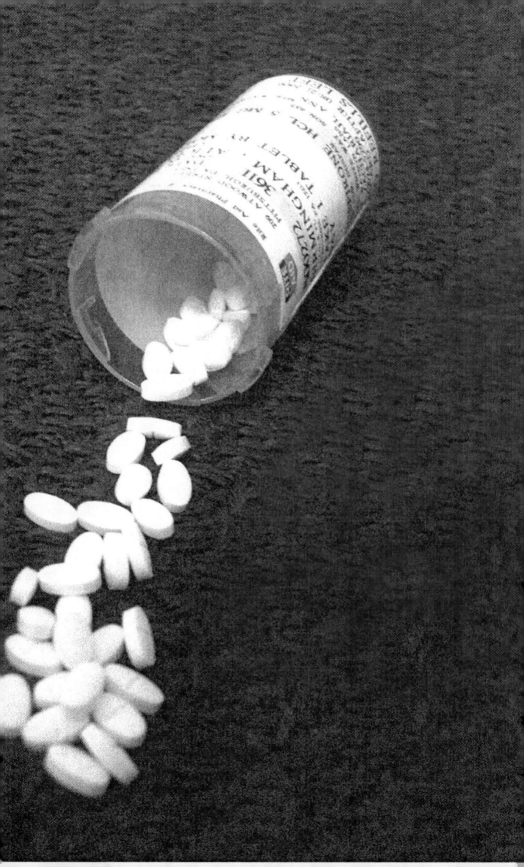

How Deep

There was a moment
when all I could see was
the color of rage
staining my world

It was the way the fine hairs
on my arms stood at attention
just waiting
for you to say the wrong thing
anything

And I found where you hid
every knife in the house

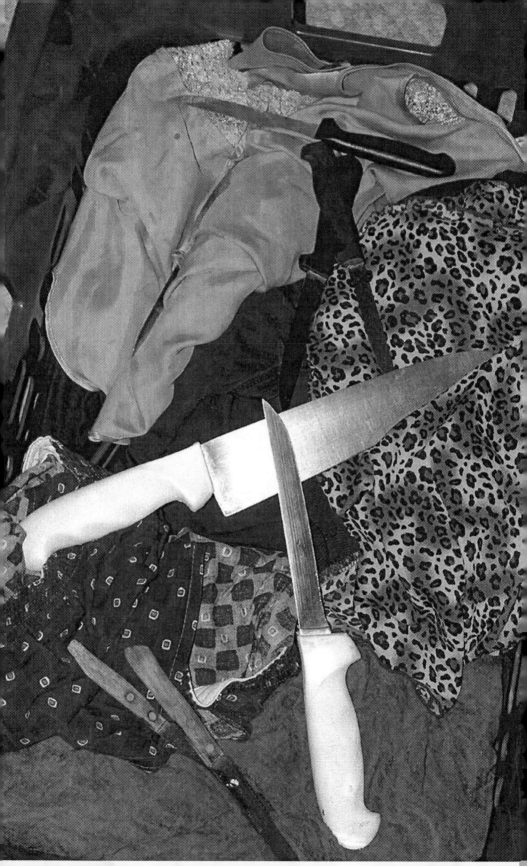

Fever

It's burning inside me
this evil
insidious
poisonous
giddy laughter
scratching at my insides
tearing my flesh
screaming
crying
dying
to get
out

photo credits: Heather Wood

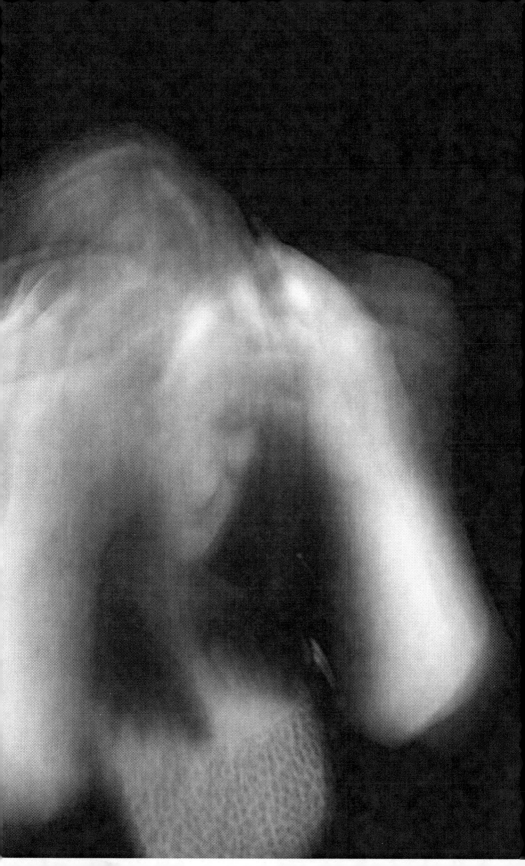

"Operation normal human being"
-Sing the Evens, Play the Odds

The 13th Floor

I'm pinned to their chairs
as they drill me
and though they ask me
a million questions
they're only interested
in two answers

"Are you going to kill yourself tonight
or (better yet) kill someone else?"

Yes
I'm sorry
I'm dreaming of swallowing
a bottle of lithium
and turning the phones off

And
I can't get the image
of stabbing my boyfriend
with a steak knife
out of my head

I'll be admitted to the
thirteenth floor
where they'll drug me
and then quiet
will settle over my chaos
and drown it all away

photo credits: Jason Bowman

Velvet Underground

My mania has splashed
like messy modern art
piss
and
watercolor
Today Andy Warhol
is my best friend

They gave me extra Geodon
last night in hopes
it would quell my most
beautiful
blossoming
morning
mania

Yet I popped out of bed
wound tight
and I can't write
because I want to dance
and I can't dance
because I want to sing
and to love everyone

Shatter

Tears burn cool
on hot flesh
sizzling
laughing
at the dazzling pain
of my existence
The way my mind
betrays
my body
and it's all shredding
my soul
How can I be pumped full of
Lithium
Depakote
Ativan
and yet my mind
rabid and ruthless
still breaks
free

MAY CAUSE DROWSINESS ALCOHOL
MAY INTENSIFY THIS EFFECT. USE
CARE WHEN OPERATING A CAR OR
DANGEROUS MACHINES

MAY CAUSE RESTLESSNESS/INSOMNIA
WARNING: DO NOT USE WHILE YOU
ARE BREASTFEEDING CONSULT YOUR
DOCTOR OR PHARMACIST

DO NOT EAT GRAPEFRUIT OR DRINK
GRAPEFRUIT JUICE AT ANYTIME
WHILE TAKING THIS MEDICATION

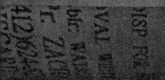 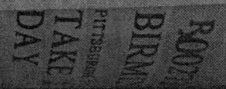

Patient Discharge

"Dangerously happy"
the nurse said
locking eyes with me
as she told the children
exactly what mania is

I sat at a table
on a unit full of teens
and young children
and me
an ancient twenty-five

It was depressing
the way each small
barren room was occupied
by another haunted soul

and numbing
in the way everything in the place was
nailed down
and the way we lined up like cattle
at the medication window

and discouraging
the way they all said
they will never be back
and the way I see them there
over and over
again

photo credits: Heather Wood

When You Don't Say the Name

There is a new patient
a paranoid schizophrenic
He is madly
truly
deeply
in love with me
He drew a picture
wrote me a romantic letter
that was about
love
a white Christmas
lottery tickets
and fried chicken
It was beautiful

Grandiose

Today
I am an amazing
fabulous
fantastical
goddess
You are lucky to lay eyes on me
to be graced by me
I'm naked
and beg you
to press yourself against my flesh
for only a moment
to feel my heat
to know my temperature
and heart beating
deep inside
quick
like a hummingbird
Tomorrow
you will know
I was there
barely a thumbprint on your cool flesh
Today I am an amazing
fabulous
fantastical
goddess

photo credits: Jason Bowman

Fly

Sometimes your feet get sick of pacing the same hall
Your eyes tire of those same four walls
the same crazy people
crying
screaming
laughing
at their situation
their lot in life
their *diagnonsense*

I'm dead drugged from the Geodon
It's keeping my
shiny
happy
mania
at bay
I feel like I would do anything
ANYTHING
to have it in my grasp right now

I miss it
no matter how desperately I cry
"Cure me, cure me NOW!"
I want that feeling
I want to fly

photo credits: Jason Bowman

Lunch

I'll bet they aren't thinking
that we're sitting here talking
about breaking chicken bones
to hurt ourselves with

But we're desperate
and would do anything
to escape this disassociation
this numb
dark
world

photo credits: Heather Wood

Bliss

Sunday morning
and I awake blessed with a calm
that has settled over my mind
like dew spread over the morning lawn

When my meds kick in
it's as if I was never ravaged
by mental illness
those wolves baying at my
heels

Until the next time
I crash
and burn
dying inside

UPMC HEALTH SYSTEM

Western Psychiatric Institute and Clinic
3811 O'Hara Street
Pittsburgh, PA 15213-2593

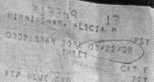
BIRMINGHAM, ALICIA M
000213369 3136 05/28/02   PSY
                                        CAT F
FEP BLUE CRO   PSY

PATIENT DISCHARGE INFORMATION

Here is some important information we've put together for you to make things easier to remember as you are discharged. Since this sheet includes reminders about appointments, phone numbers and medicine, you'll want to keep in a handy place for easy reference. We hope you'll find it helpful.

 UPMC HEALTH SYSTEM

Western Psychiatric Institute and Clinic
3811 O'Hara Street
Pittsburgh, PA 15213-2593

BIRMINGHAM, ALICIA M
000213369 3137 05/17/03   PSY

PRIVATE PAY   12/05/79   23Y

PATIENT DISCHARGE INFORMATION

Here is some important information we've put together for you to make things easier to remember as you are discharged. Since this sheet includes reminders about appointments, phone numbers and medicine, you'll want to keep in a handy place for easy reference. We hope you'll find it helpful.

  UPMC HEALTH SYSTEM

Western Psychiatric Institute and Clinic
3811 O'Hara Street
Pittsburgh, PA 15213-2593

ALLEGHENY CO. EMERGENCY
SERVICES (A.C.E.S.)

213369   7
BIRMINGHAM, ALICIA M
000213369 4086 03/26/04   PSY
                                     NOR F
PRIVATE PAY   12/05/79   24Y

PATIENT DISCHARGE INFORMATION

IMPRINT PATIENT IDENTIFICATION HERE

Here is some important information we've put together for you to make things easier to remember as you are discharged. Since this sheet includes reminders about appointments, phone numbers and medicine, you'll want to keep in a handy place for easy reference. We hope you'll find it helpful.

Your Treatment Team (Unit: ___CPA II   7th floor___

YOUR NEXT APPOINTMENT

Your first outpatient appointment is ___Tues 4/16/04___ at ___11:30___ a.m. / pm.

You will be seen in ___ Your clinician will be ___

The clinic is located ___↳ Adult Clinic___   ___business___

Should you need to reach your clinician before your first appointment, you can call the clinician between

___hrs___ at the following number(s) ___

Please feel free to call you clinician if any questions or problems arise before your first appointment. It is especially important to call if you are unable to keep your first appointment. Your clinician will be glad to reschedule your appointment if that becomes necessary.

In case of any emergency, after clinic hours, staff is available 24 hours/day in the Diagnostic and Evaluation Center (DEC). The DEC telephone number is ◆◆◆

Your local mental health center is ___WPIC___   at ___ (phone)

Please call ___ (case manager)

if you have any questions or concerns

YOUR MEDICATION

If medication has been ordered for you, it is because the medicine is know to be helpful to people with similar problems, and is thought to be essential to your recover. It is important for you to take these medicines as prescribed. Your nurse has discussed your medications with you and if you have any questions about the medications or their side effects, please discuss your concerns with your clinician.

The medication you are taking is:
Geodon   100 mg
Lithium   600 mg
               450 mg

Medication Schedule:
at bedtime
in Am + at bedtime
at noon

Special Instructions:

ADDITIONAL FOLLOW-UP

Ink

Words are muffled
by the bone white hair of the nurse
sitting
staring
I know she hates me
From this meeting
I get the idea I can go home
by the middle of next week
My thoughts are no longer
flowing like mercury
something my pen misses
but my mind sings grateful praises for-
the calm a higher dose brings
a calm that frustrates my pen just enough

I have to wonder
what my boyfriend wants to hear from me
what it is he'd like my ink to spill forth
No doubt something sound
wholesome
well-adjusted
something that isn't reflective of these
stark
white
walls
free of mirrors
free of freedom

photo credits: Jason Bowman

2001

I could see the longing
the way thoughts of suicide
danced behind his eyes
any hope of healing smashed by
the weight of his psychotic depression

One day he said to me
the saddest thing I've ever heard
"You have the most beautiful face
I've ever seen.
I'm going to kill myself
in three days."

But after pacing the halls for hours
and trying to stab himself with my pen
it's a shot of 5 mgs of Ativan
as he struggles in the rubber room
with the demons that live
just under
the skin

photo credits: Heather Wood

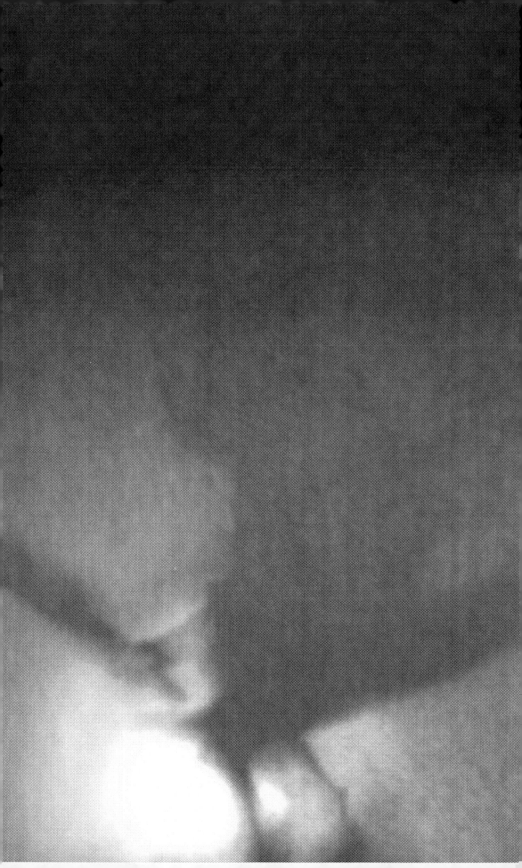

"Where has all the passion gone"
-The Relapse

11:00 AM 75 degrees

"Sorry, Miss but you don't have an appointment."

"Please, please, please..."
I didn't mean to break
sanity slowly seeping from my wounds
when it was inconvenient for you

"When were you discharged from the hospital?"

I respond with silence
You and your glaring eyes are nothing to me
and everything
yet you don't even know I'm here

"You seem sad."

Words I hear falling from your lips
as I imagine they will 1,000 times today
meaningless
empty
I wonder if you remember my name

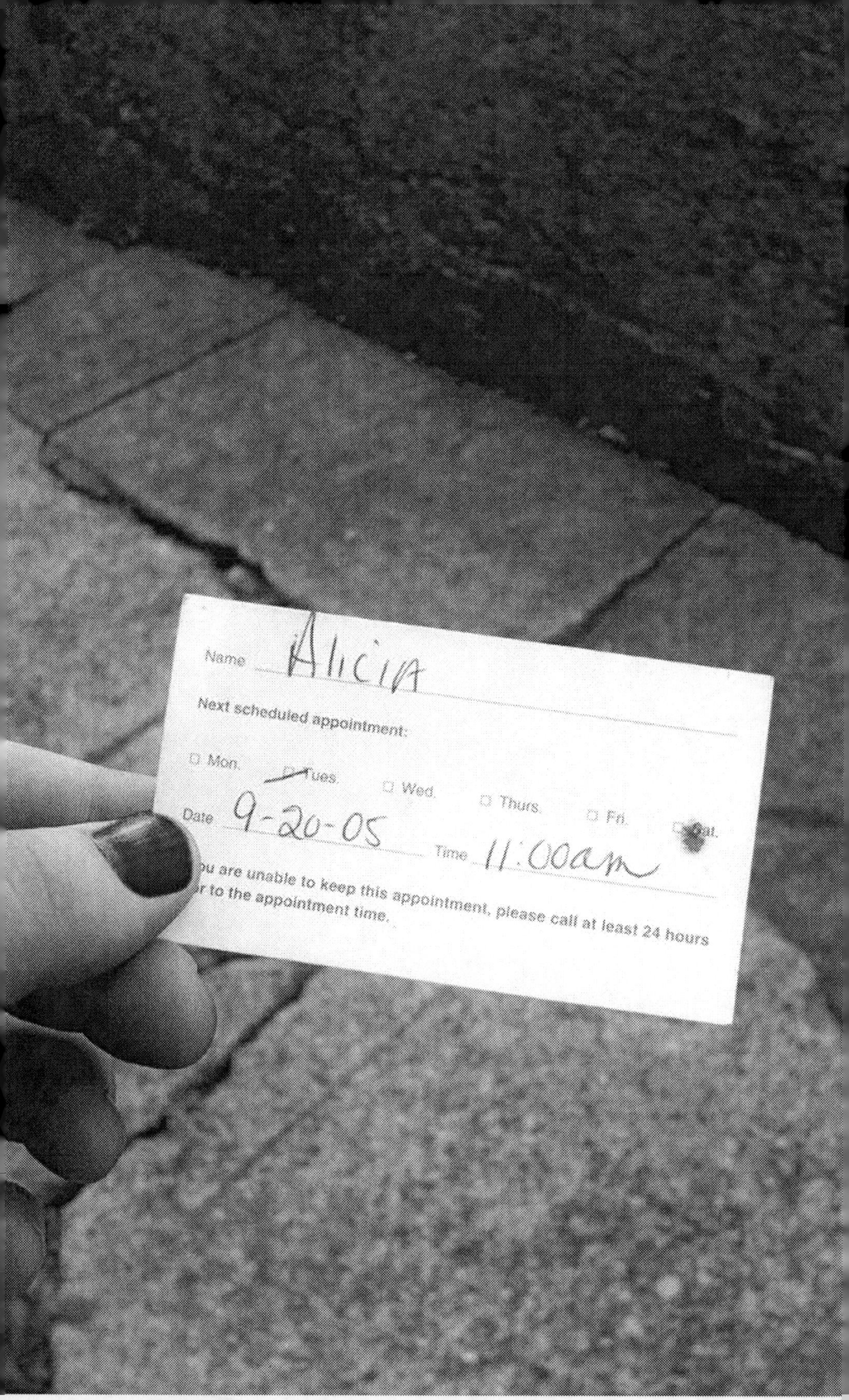
Name Alicia
Next scheduled appointment:
Mon.
Tues.
Wed.
Thurs.
Fri.
Sat.
Date 9-20-05
Time 11:00am
ou are unable to keep this appointment, please call at least 24 hours
r to the appointment time.

Untitled

My body
burdened by the weight
of my melancholy
can't be peeled
off the floor

I've never ached
with such agony
carrying this
unbearable
intolerable
oppressive pain

The tears come
Yet they can't wash it away

photo credits: Jason Bowman

Black Water

I sit ravaged
turning the bath water
a deep shade
of shame
filling my personal ocean
with black water
like velvet
touching you torn

I listen for my lover
in the next room
as I beg for someone
anyone
to stop me
to hold me
to heal me

photo credits: Jason Bowman

Goodnight

I see the disappointment
splashed all over your face
the way you can't stand
another day of my mind
breaking before you

Your pitying smile is warm
like a kiss on the forehead
as I slip into bed
but I see the part of you
that regrets me

A kiss goodnight and I fill you
with empty promises
that this time
again
will be the last

Baby's Breath

Like baby's breath
choking the rose
you hold me
while I crumble before you
my soul slipping through your fingers
empty and alone

You tell me
everything will be alright
and I wish I were weeping
but the tears won't come

I tell you
I can fake it
and that I'm fine
because that is what
you want to hear

And I dance
spinning and twirling
and I say baby
baby I'm fine

photo credits: Heather Wood

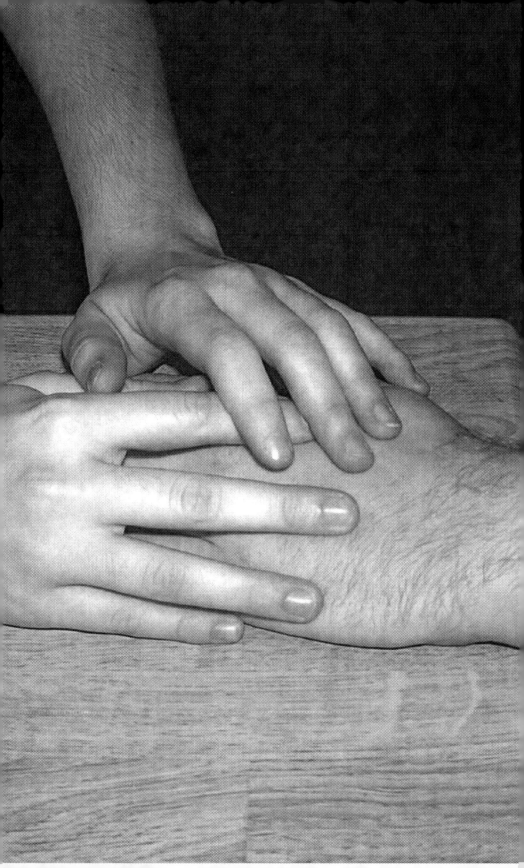

DJB

Papap always said they would come for me

You say
we can make it
that you can
wade through this mess
I've made of my life
You say you won't leave
that my crazy
won't invade you

Yet I know it won't be easy
and there will be 26 hour days
with no sleep in sight
as you wait again
for the men in the little white suits
to come and take me away

Smashing

I gut myself
tearing out all the hate inside
Sometimes I wonder
what will be left of me
after it's all over

Tears want to come
banging behind my eyes
smashing through to the surface
burning away the guilt of my sin
to leave this world behind with no good-byes

photo credits: Jason Bowman

First

It was as if in that one
unguarded moment
something crept in
something sinister
someone
anyone
but me

There was a compulsion
I cried while I listened to Mike Ness croon
"Would you compromise and realize
the price was too much to pay"
while I swallowed sobs and pills
honestly not knowing why

I lowered myself fully clothed into the bath tub
Warmth soaked my soul
driving away the icy mournful sobs of suicide
I waited for sleep to come
for dirty bathwater to fill my lungs
A guarantee I'd never see the inside of a hospital
or the mania rushing toward me again

photo credits: Alicia Birmingham

Déjà vu

My eyes follow
the green and pink
institutional colors
as they drip down the walls
spilling into puddles of madness
and drowning us all in this place's
cheap brand of mental health

I can feel the way one person's
insanity seeps into another
The way the bipolars feed off
the beautiful spiraling mania
and the sinking depression

I knock on the door
to the medication room
and you watch
as I swallow
another
pink pill
medicating
my crazy
away

"We've come too far now to die"
-Shiver

Ode to Rite Aid

It seems an eternity
that you've held my hand
through the quiet madness
through the not so quiet madness

I'm walking away from my rock today
walking away from years
of a steady
enduring
abiding home

Tears that haven't escaped me for years
now burn scars into my soul
I step away to turn and say
good-bye
To turn and say
I would have never made it
without you

Fated

Today is a good day

One of those days
when you let yourself forget
that you overdosed 18 days ago
and you just spent the last two weeks
in the hospital
waiting for medication to seep in
and make your
crazy
sane

One of those days
when you think
this will last forever
even though you know
spring is coming
and mania will soon follow
but it feels like
eternity
today

photo credits: Marilyn Jean Wood

Remission

Staring at this blank screen
I can't help but wonder
where my muse has gone
She's abandoned me
or perhaps I killed her
poisoned her with some
Lithium
Geodon
Trileptal
Ativan
Perhaps that's it

I long for the days when
my words spilled like ink
and I let my fingers work
begging
searching
stretching
for all they're worth
trying to find words to
enchant
bewitch
beguile
yet I come up
empty handed

I could call her back to me
flushing my salvation
down the toilet
watching the rainbow swirl away
and yet I
shouldn't
couldn't
won't
let my life slip away from me
for nothing more than some pretty words
d a n c i n g   a c r o s s   m y   p a g e

photo credits: Jason Bowman

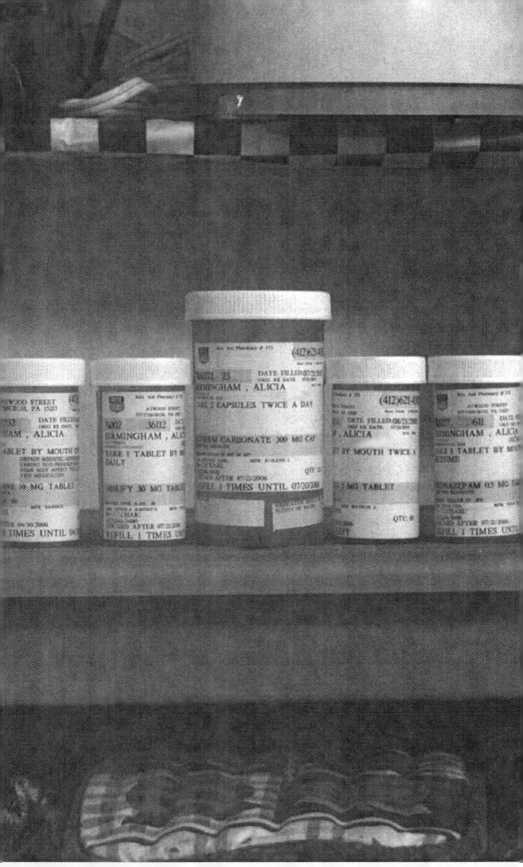

Today

Today
the landscape of my life is still
Everyday I have to reach out and touch it
just to see if it's real
My fingers come back wet
from this painting of my life

It's so new
fresh and raw
this stability that I've never known
Yet my past haunts me
I wonder to myself
who is this girl
standing here
fingers wet
pressed against the pulse of her life

Who is this girl
alive and full of a passion
that does not burn away her very soul
that rejuvenates her spirit
with every mornings breath
and every moment that does not carry with it
the regrets and mistakes
The Crazy Inside

photo credits: Jason Bowman

"When you understand that what you're telling is just a story, it isn't happening anymore. When you realize the story you're telling is just words, when you can just crumble it up and throw your past in the trashcan... then we'll figure out who you're going to be."
-Chuck Palahniuk, Invisible Monsters

ONLINE BIPOLAR RESOURCES

www.bipolar.com

www.bipolar.about.com

www.pendulum.org

www.nimh.nih.gov/publicat/bipolar.cfm

www.webmd.com

www.bpkids.org

www.afsp.org

FREE MEDICATION FOR LOW INCOME PEOPLE

www.needymeds.com

www.themedicineprogram.com

BIPOLAR DISORDER BOOKS

The Bipolar Disorder Survival Guide
-David J. Miklowitz

Loving Someone With Bipolar Disorder
-Julie A. Fast, John D. Preston

Bipolar Disorder: A Guide for Patients and Families
-Francis Mark Mondimore M.D

An Unquiet Mind: A Memoir of Moods and Madness
-Kay Redfield Jamison

Electroboy: A Memoir of Mania
-Andy Behrmen

If you are suicidal, get help now.
1-800-suicide

Printed in the United States
100163LV00004B/519/A